LIVE LIKE A

VIKING

DISCOVERING THE SECRETS OF THE VIKINGS

CLAIRE SAUNDERS

ILLUSTRATED BY
RUTH HICKSON

Button
BOOKS

CONTENTS

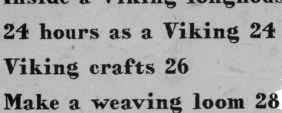

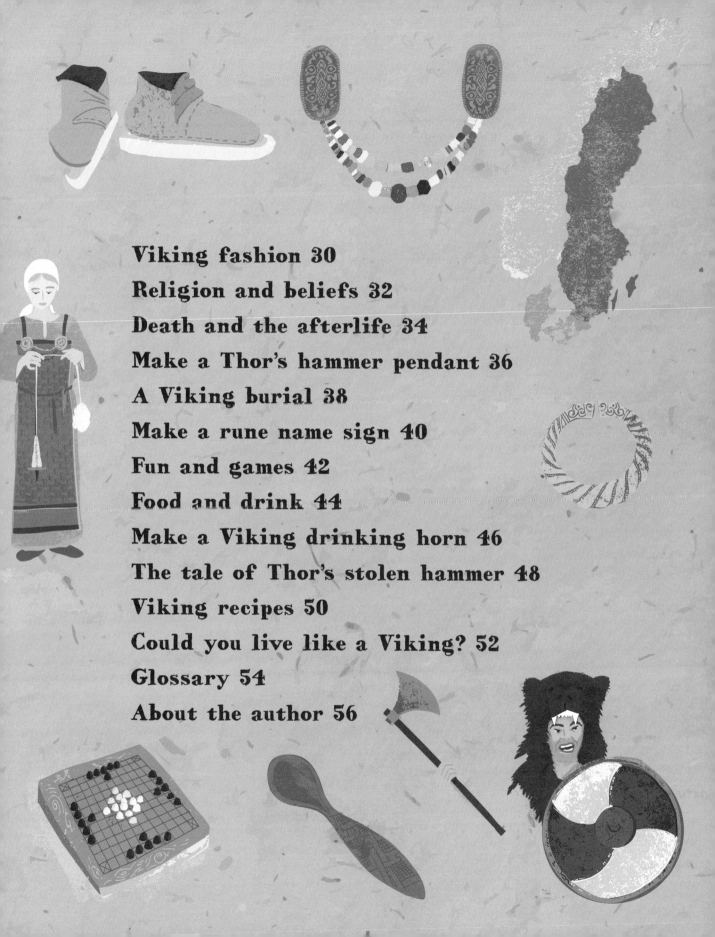

WHO WERE THE VIKINGS?

Around 1,200 years ago, people from Scandinavia in the far north of Europe began crossing the sea to raid neighbouring lands, killing and stealing treasure. These fierce seafaring raiders were Vikings, and their hit-and-run attacks on peaceful villages and monasteries spread terror throughout Europe.

Scandinavia

Norway

Sweden

Denmark

Raiders, traders and farmers

Not all Vikings who left their homelands were bloodthirsty raiders in search of loot and adventure. Some came to foreign lands to settle peacefully as farmers or craftspeople. Others were merchants who traded goods all over Europe, from Russia to the Middle East. The Vikings were also great explorers, whose epic voyages led them to distant lands far across the ocean.

A Viking friend

My name is Astrid and I have lived for ten summers. My home is a small farming village, not far from the sea. Every year, when the days start getting longer, my father and older brothers pack up their belongings and go raiding. Summer is almost over now, and soon it will be time for them to return, if the gods will it. I can't wait to hear about their adventures! I have stories of my own to share too, about life on the farm. Come with me and let me tell you how I live.

4

Myth busting

How do you imagine the Vikings? Here are some common myths:

They spent all their time looting and fighting

Most Vikings were actually peaceful farmers, craftworkers or traders. Even the Vikings that did go raiding didn't do it all the time. In between raids, they returned home to look after their farms.

They were uncivilized, lawless savages

The Vikings listened to music and poetry and were skilled craftworkers. Society was governed by strict laws, and Viking women had more freedom than women in many other societies of the time.

They were one group of people

The Vikings weren't a single nation. They were small, separate groups of people, with their own local rulers. But they shared a similar culture, language (called Old Norse) and religion. For a long time the Vikings were pagans, unlike many other people living in Europe at that time, who were Christians.

Viking writing

They wore big horns on their helmets

There's no evidence for this. This myth was probably invented in the 1800s.

Sea Raider

The word 'Viking' means 'sea raider'. The Vikings were master sailors — experts at navigating their homeland's rocky coastlines and narrow fjords (inlets). They were known by other names too, including Norsemen ('men of the north'), Danes and Rus.

TIMELINE OF THE VIKINGS

The Viking Age lasted for around 300 years, from the 8th to the 11th centuries. At first, the Vikings carried out quick, surprise raids on foreign shores, before returning home with their loot. Later, they began to settle in some places, eventually becoming part of the local population.

793 CE
One of the first Viking raids is an attack on Lindisfarne monastery on the English coast. Soon, Vikings are making raids all over Britain and Ireland.

840s and 850s
Viking raiders reach Spain and North Africa. In 860, they attack Constantinople (now Istanbul).

870s
Norwegian Vikings begin to settle in Iceland. They bring cattle, sheep and goats with them in their ships.

Jorvik (York)

865
The Great Heathen Army, an alliance of thousands of Viking warriors, conquers much of central Britain.

845
The Vikings attack Paris, France. They are paid gold and silver to leave.

870s
The area of Britain controlled by Vikings becomes known as the Danelaw. Jorvik (York) is its most important city. Scandinavian settlers looking for better farmland migrate to Britain.

c.965
Denmark becomes Christian under King Harold 'Bluetooth'. Norway and Sweden follow later.

Greenland

North America

c. 1000
Erik the Red's son, Leif the Lucky, crosses the Atlantic and lands in Newfoundland. He is the first European to reach North America.

1066
Harold Hardrada, King of Norway, claims the English throne but is defeated by the English King Harold at Stamford Bridge. Later that year, Harold is himself defeated by William the Conqueror at the Battle of Hastings. William the Conqueror is the great, great, great grandson of a Viking called Rollo (see box, below).

981–985
When Erik the Red is banished from Iceland, he sails west and founds a settlement in Greenland.

1019–35
The whole of England is ruled by the Viking king of Denmark and Norway, Cnut (also known as Canute).

Famous Vikings

Ragnar Lothbrok (800s)

Legendary Danish king and fierce raider, who may or may not have actually existed. Lothbrok means 'Hairy Breeches'!

Rollo (died c. 930)

Warrior who became the first ruler of Normandy in France. Said to be too huge to ride a horse, he had to walk instead.

Freydis Eiríksdóttir (died c. 1004)

The brave daughter of Erik the Red. In one story, she fought off a group of attackers single-handed, while all the Viking men ran away.

Greenland

Vinland
(North America)

Iceland

L'Anse aux
Meadows

Cuerdale hoard, England
This impressive Viking treasure
trove contained over 8,600
items, including silver coins
and jewellery.

Atlantic Ocean

Ireland   Jo:
(Y

Dublin

Brit:

MAP OF THE VIKING WORLD

This map shows where the Vikings raided, traded and
settled, and some of the monuments and treasures they
left behind. Generally, the Vikings from Norway and
Denmark sailed west, towards Britain and beyond.
Those from Sweden mainly explored eastwards, using
rivers to travel into Russia and towards Constantinople.

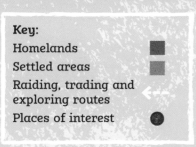

Key:
Homelands
Settled areas
Raiding, trading and
exploring routes
Places of interest

Viking homelands
Timber
Iron
Animal skins and fur
Walrus tusks

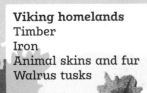

**Borg longhouse,
Lofoten islands, Norway**
This huge, 272ft (83m) long
chieftain's longhouse is the largest
Viking house ever discovered.

Russia/Persia
Silk
Furs
Spices
Glassware
Semi-precious stones

Sweden

Russia

orway

Birka

Novgorod

Novgorod, Russia
Viking sledges have been found
in Novgorod in Russia. The
Vikings might have used horse-
drawn sledges to travel along
frozen rivers in winter.

Northern Europe
Slaves
Metal
Cloth

Hedeby

Denmark

**Constantinople
(modern-day Istanbul, Turkey)**
The capital of the Byzantine
Empire was known to the
Vikings as Miklagård ('the great
city'). One Viking visitor left
some graffiti behind: it says
'Halvdan Was Here'.

Lindholm Høje, Denmark
Some of the stone markers
in this Viking graveyard
are arranged into the
shape of ships.

Oseberg longship, Norway
This magnificent longship was
discovered in a burial mound.

France

Southern Europe
Pottery
Wine
Salt

**Mediterranean
Sea**

Trading

The Vikings traded all over
Europe. The map shows some
of the goods they bought and
sold. Some settlements, such
as Birka in Sweden, Hedeby in
Denmark and Jorvik in
England, became important
Viking trading centres.

A trader's set
of scales

Africa

VIKING LONGSHIPS

The Vikings were superb sailors and master ship-builders. They sailed all kinds of boats, from small fishing boats to large, sturdy cargo ships called knarrs, but they are most famous for their longships. These long, narrow boats were swift, agile and light – perfect for quick coastal raids. Sailing at speeds of up to 11 mph (18 kph), they were much faster than other ships of the time. In good conditions, a ship could make the voyage from Norway to England in less than two days.

The carved, wooden figurehead at the front of the longship might show a dragon or serpent head, to strike fear into the enemy.

At sea

The Vikings didn't have compasses to help them navigate. Where possible, they sailed along the coast, keeping sight of land. When they headed off into the open sea, they probably navigated using the sun and stars, as well as their knowledge of waves, currents and seabirds.

When there was not enough wind for sailing, oars were used instead. The rowers probably sat on sea chests that held their belongings.

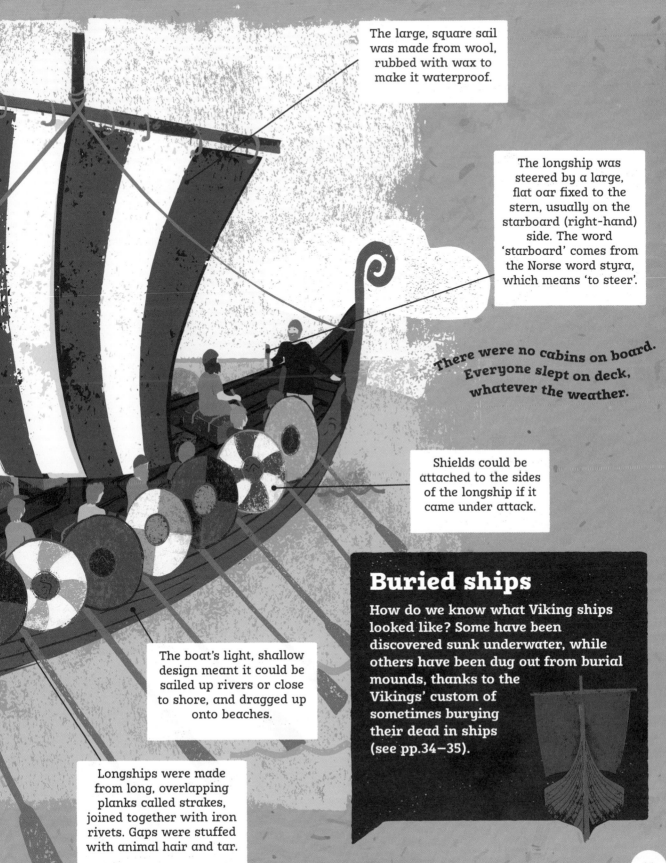

The large, square sail was made from wool, rubbed with wax to make it waterproof.

The longship was steered by a large, flat oar fixed to the stern, usually on the starboard (right-hand) side. The word 'starboard' comes from the Norse word styra, which means 'to steer'.

There were no cabins on board. Everyone slept on deck, whatever the weather.

Shields could be attached to the sides of the longship if it came under attack.

The boat's light, shallow design meant it could be sailed up rivers or close to shore, and dragged up onto beaches.

Longships were made from long, overlapping planks called strakes, joined together with iron rivets. Gaps were stuffed with animal hair and tar.

Buried ships

How do we know what Viking ships looked like? Some have been discovered sunk underwater, while others have been dug out from burial mounds, thanks to the Vikings' custom of sometimes burying their dead in ships (see pp.34−35).

ATTACK!

Viking raids were swift and savage. Once the longships reached land, warriors swarmed ashore, setting buildings ablaze and looting anything valuable. Caught by surprise, the terrified local people had no time to prepare or escape, and many were murdered or captured as slaves. No wonder the Vikings were so feared.

Tactics

Early raiding expeditions were usually made up of a small number of boats, which sailed along the coast or up rivers, striking with no warning before making a quick get-away. Later, the Vikings began to set up camps and organised themselves into armies. Sometimes their families went with them on campaigns.

The Vikings fought mainly on foot. Battles began with a shower of spears, arrows and stones, before the men moved in to fight hand-to-hand, swinging their battle-axes and swords. Strength, courage and loyalty were prized above all else.

Local rulers sometimes paid the Vikings money called 'Danegeld' to stay away and leave them in peace.

Berserkers

If you think Viking fighters sound terrifying, you wouldn't want to meet a berserker! The Viking sagas describe how these warriors, dressed in nothing but bearskins, worked themselves up into a frenzy of rage, biting their shields and howling, before charging fearlessly into battle. They believed that Odin, the god of war, protected them and gave them superhuman powers.

Viking warriors

A Viking could be called on by their chieftain or king to go raiding or into battle at any time. Men had to supply their own weapons, and most fought using spears or axes. Only rich Vikings could afford swords. These were a sign of status and a prized possession, handed down from father to son. Some were even praised in poems and given names, such as 'Leg-biter'.

Chieftain

Helmet with nose guard

Chainmail shirts took a long time to make, so were expensive. A mail shirt might cost the same as two horses.

Padded leather, to protect the body

Axe

Double-edged sword (sharp on both edges), with leather scabbard

Ordinary warrior

Leather cap

Brightly painted, large, round shield

Skilful spear-throwers were said to be able to throw two spears at once, one from each hand!

THE RAIDERS RETURN

I am weaving with my mother when we suddenly hear shouting outside. I jump up, dropping my spindle, just as my older sister, Frida, bursts into the house, pink-cheeked and panting. 'They're back!' she cries, 'Come quickly!' My heart hammering in my chest, I run with my mother to the top of the field. Here we can see the glinting sky-blue sea spread out in front of us, smooth as a blanket. Sure enough, in the distance I spot a brightly coloured sail! The men are finally returning from their summer's raiding!

Quickly, I call my younger brothers and sisters and we hurry down to the shore, where our neighbours are beginning to gather. As I watch the ship draw closer, my heart is in my mouth. Please let my father and brother be safe on board! Last autumn, my friend Inga's brother did not return – he was hit by an arrow on a raid, and the wound never healed.

Soon the wait is over. The ship glides to the shore and my father leaps over the side, sunburnt and smiling from ear to ear. I run towards him and he swings me up high up into the air. 'How is my little Astrid?' he laughs, squeezing me so tight I can hardly breathe. My mother wraps her arms around my brother, Ulf, fretting over a new scar on his forehead. All around me people are laughing, shouting, hugging.

We all help to unload the ship. There are battered sea chests, axes and dented shields, and heavy, bulging sacks damp with sea spray. At the back of the ship I can see a few people huddled together in chains, looking tired and scared – new slaves to help in the fields. I peek into one of the sacks and catch a glimpse of a gleaming cross on a thick golden chain, before the bag is whisked away from me. Later, there will be a feast and we will gaze in wonder at all the treasures our fearless men have brought back. I can't wait to hear their stories about the battles they have fought! No one is braver than my father.

My mother tells me to head home and help prepare food for the feast, so I link arms with Ulf and we wander back towards the farm. As we walk, he tells me about monasteries full of incredible riches, about a fierce storm at sea that lasted for three whole days, about villages burnt to the ground and about fearsome battles. But he also tells me about the farmland he has seen across the ocean – fields of plump corn and pastures grazed by more sheep than you can count. One day, he tells me, he will sail across the sea and make his home in this new land. Maybe I could cross the ocean with him, I think happily. What an adventure that would be!

VIKING SOCIETY

There was no central government in the Viking kingdoms. For many years, regions were ruled by different kings, with the help of powerful local chieftains. The men in charge expected loyalty from the people under them, and in return they granted them favours.

Jarls, karls and thralls

This pyramid shows the different classes of Viking society:

Chieftains, or jarls, were in charge of smaller local areas. They owned land and ships, and had the power to call up the local men to join them in raids or in battle. Loyalty to the chieftain was rewarded with feasts, honour and a share of the loot. Chieftains with a lot of wealth and influence might become kings.

Thralls, or slaves, had no rights at all. Most thralls were captured in raids or bought by traders, but some were karls who had committed a crime. Life for thralls was tough – if their owner died, they might even be killed and buried with them. But sometimes a slave could buy their freedom or be freed by their owner.

Kings ruled over large areas of land, helped by local chieftains. They became more powerful over time. Eventually, Norway, Sweden and Denmark were each ruled by a single king.

Most Vikings were **karls**. These were ordinary people who mostly worked as farmers or craftworkers. Some were poor and some were well off. Going on raids with the local chieftain was a good way to get richer!

Kings

Jarls

Karls

Thralls

Law and order

The Vikings decided on laws and judged crimes at local assemblies called Things. These meetings were led by someone called a lawspeaker, and all free men (but not women) could attend them. As kings became more powerful in Scandinavia, Things became less common.

Punishments for law-breakers included paying a fine to the victim, called Wergild, or being cast out of the community as an outlaw. Most outlaws could not survive alone and died.

Sometimes disputes were settled with a fight known as Holmgang. The Vikings believed the gods would make sure the person who was in the right would win the fight.

In Iceland, the Vikings set up a Thing called the Althing, which is still going today. It's said to be the world's oldest parliament.

Honour

Honour and reputation were very important to the Vikings. People were expected to be loyal to their family, to the local chieftain and to the men they fought alongside. They believed that oaths (promises) must be kept, and any wrongdoing had to be avenged.

FAMILY LIFE

Men made all the rules in Viking society, but in the home it was the women who were in charge. It was their job to provide food and make clothes for the family, and to look after the farm when the men were off raiding.

Women's rights

Viking women didn't have equal rights to men, but they were respected and had more freedoms than other women living at the time. A woman could own property and choose to divorce her husband if she wanted to. Some crossed the ocean with their husbands and families to help start new settlements abroad.

Fierce women warriors appear in Viking stories, but archaeologists don't think most women actually fought in battle.

Childhood

Children grew up quickly. There was no school. Instead, children helped out around the house and the farm, learning all the skills they would need as adults, from farming to fighting. By the time they were teenagers, they were ready to run a farm and a household. Girls normally married very young.

Toys

Children played with homemade toys carved from wood or bone. Some toys, such as wooden swords, helped children learn skills they would need as adults. Archaeologists have even found miniature toy versions of lamps and other household objects.

Viking names

After a baby was born, they became part of the family at a special ceremony, where they were sprinkled with water and given a name.

Names had special meanings. Astrid, for instance, meant 'beautiful and loved'. Boys might be named after the god Thor, or fierce animals such as bears (Bjorn) or wolves (Ulf). Some people also had nicknames, called bynames, which might describe how they looked or behaved. How do you think Sweyn Forkbeard, Thorfinn Skull-Splitter and Eysteinn Foul-Fart got their nicknames?

VIKING SETTLEMENTS

Most Vikings were farmers, who lived in remote homesteads or little villages made up of a handful of farms. There were also a few small towns, mainly on the coast. These were important centres for trade, and were home to merchants and craftsmen.

Each farm had a longhouse, where the family lived. Smaller buildings were used for workshops, food stores, byres (cattle sheds) and slaves' housing. Some farms had their own smithy.

People foraged for fruit, berries and nuts, and caught fish and shellfish in the sea and rivers. Some Vikings also hunted.

People walked, or drove carts pulled by horses or oxen. In winter, they zipped about on skis or used horse-drawn sledges.

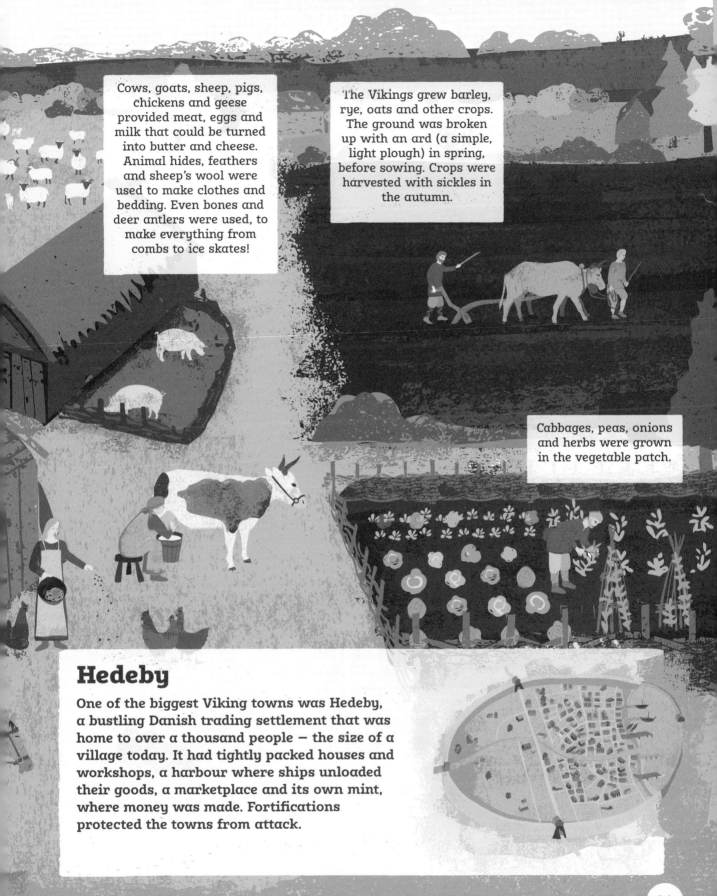

Cows, goats, sheep, pigs, chickens and geese provided meat, eggs and milk that could be turned into butter and cheese. Animal hides, feathers and sheep's wool were used to make clothes and bedding. Even bones and deer antlers were used, to make everything from combs to ice skates!

The Vikings grew barley, rye, oats and other crops. The ground was broken up with an ard (a simple, light plough) in spring, before sowing. Crops were harvested with sickles in the autumn.

Cabbages, peas, onions and herbs were grown in the vegetable patch.

Hedeby

One of the biggest Viking towns was Hedeby, a bustling Danish trading settlement that was home to over a thousand people – the size of a village today. It had tightly packed houses and workshops, a harbour where ships unloaded their goods, a marketplace and its own mint, where money was made. Fortifications protected the towns from attack.

INSIDE A VIKING LONGHOUSE

On Viking farms, children, parents, grandparents and other relatives all lived together in a large rectangular building called a longhouse. This was usually just one big room, where people slept, worked, prepared food, ate and played. It would have been crowded, noisy and smelly!

1 The toilet was just a hole in the ground outside. Household waste, such as bones, was probably thrown onto rubbish heaps called middens.

2 Homes were made cosier with furs, animal skins and feather-filled cushions. Blankets and wall hangings were woven on a big loom by the women of the house.

3 A firepit in the centre of the longhouse was used for cooking and heating, and the fire was kept burning all day. There was no chimney. Some smoke escaped through a hole in the roof, but the longhouse would still have been very smoky.

4 Windows were rare. The only light came from the fire and simple oil lamps.

5 Household goods and valuables were stored in lockable chests.

6 Longhouses were built using local materials. Walls were usually made of wooden planks, stone or wattle-and-daub (woven sticks plastered with a sticky mud mixture). The roof was thatched or covered with turf to make it waterproof.

7 The floor was stamped-down earth, which sometimes had straw or ashes from the fire scattered over it.

8 Wide benches ran around the walls. People sat and slept on these, away from the chilly draughts by the floor. Most people had very little furniture, other than a few low stools. Only rich Vikings had beds and chairs.

9 Some longhouses had a byre (animal shed) at one end. Cattle would be kept there during the cold winter months.

Imagine!

Close your eyes and imagine all the smells in a longhouse: smoke from the fire, a stew simmering over it, fish oil burning in the lamps, animal dung and plenty of unwashed humans!

In towns, where there was less space, houses were smaller.

Turf houses

In Iceland and other parts of the Viking world, wood was hard to come by, so people covered the longhouse walls and roof with turf instead.

24 HOURS AS A VIKING

There was always lots of work to be done on a Viking farm, and children were expected to do their fair share! This is what might have happened to Astrid on a typical day.

6am: wake up

Astrid wakes up when the cockerel crows at dawn. Her first job is getting the fire going. In the half-light, she stumbles over to the hearth and feeds the warm embers with twigs. Soon, a small fire is blazing.

6.30am: breakfast

There's some leftover stew from last night in the cooking pot, so she scoops some out and eats it with a hunk of stale bread and a cup of buttermilk.

7am: morning jobs

Astrid starts her morning jobs. She gathers up the eggs laid by the chickens and geese, then waters the vegetable patch. Afterwards, she and her siblings take turns grinding grain into flour using a heavy quern-stone. Phew, it's hard work! She'll help her mother make bread with the flour tomorrow.

10am: foraging

It's a sunny day, so her mother sends her out to gather berries, nuts and firewood with her siblings. They find juicy raspberries, hazelnuts and plump mushrooms.

1pm: spinning wool

While her brothers are practising sword-fighting outside, Astrid picks up a basket of sheep's wool and helps her grandmother spin it into thread.

3pm: preparing dinner

A neighbour has popped round with some fish he has just caught. Astrid's mum gives him some freshly-made cheese in return. Astrid helps her mum chop up the fish and add it to the evening's stew, which is bubbling on the fire.

6pm: bathing

After dinner, it's time for Astrid's weekly bath. She hops in a tub filled with water that's been heated over the fire, and scrubs herself with soap made from animal fat and wood ash. Everyone in her family will share the bath water.

6.30pm: evening

There's time for a quick game by the fire before bed. Astrid's father is teaching her how to play a fun board game called hnefatafl.

8pm: bedtime

It's getting dark now. Astrid snuggles up under a blanket and cosy furs while her father tells her a story about Thor and his legendary hammer. Soon she's fast asleep.

How did Vikings tell the time?

We divide our days into 24 hours, but the Vikings divided their days into eight equal parts. They could tell which part of the day they were in by noticing where the sun stood in the sky in relation to landmarks on the horizon. The middle of the day, when the sun was highest in the sky, was called 'Highday' or 'Midday'.

VIKING CRAFTS

Every object or tool that the Vikings used had to be handmade by someone. Textiles and simple objects could be made in the home. But other items were created by skilled craftspeople such as carpenters, metalworkers, and bone and antler workers.

Materials

Viking craftspeople worked with many different materials. Some of these, like wood, iron and bone, came from the local area. Others were imported from far-away countries, such as the glass used to make beads.

Stonemasons carved and painted memorial stones (see page 34).

Wooden spoon

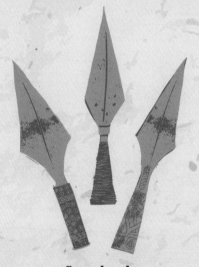

Spearheads

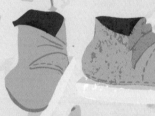

Ice skates

Wood

Most everyday objects were made from wood: chests, looms, stools, cups and spoons, games boards, tools, shields, musical instruments, wagons, ploughs, boats, and more! Carpenters often decorated their creations with beautiful carvings.

Metal

The blacksmith was an important person in Viking society. Everybody needed the useful things he made, from nails and locks to knives and cauldrons. Weaponsmiths (men who made weapons) were especially respected.

Bone and antler

Farmers might use leftover animal bones to make everything from needles to ice skates. But more ornate items, like beautifully decorated combs or knife handles, were carved by skilled bone and antler workers.

Making textiles

Making textiles was usually a woman's job. Here's how it was done:

Raw materials

Woollen cloth started out as sheep's wool. First, the wool was washed and combed.

Linen cloth was made using the flax plant. Fibres were removed from the stalk, and then combed into long thin strands.

Process

1 The wool or flax was spun. A tool called a spindle twisted the wool or flax fibres into long lengths of yarn.

2 Yarn could be dyed using natural dyes. Blue dye came from the woad plant, red from the root of the madder plant, and brown from walnut shells.

3 The yarn was woven into cloth on a wooden frame called a loom. Colourful patterns could be created by using different coloured yarns.

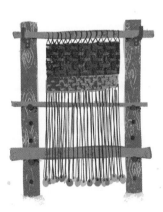

4 When it was finished, the cloth was cut with scissors, and sewn using needles made from bone. Women could 'iron' the cloth by placing it on a board and then rubbing it with a glass stone to make it smooth.

MAKE A WEAVING LOOM

Viking women were expert weavers. They made all of their family's clothes, as well as sails for ships, blankets and other textiles. Have a go at weaving yourself, using a simple cardboard loom.

Warp and weft

All looms work in the same way, by weaving together warp threads and weft threads. **WARP** threads run vertically and are fixed to the loom. The horizontal **WEFT** threads are threaded over and under the warp, creating the woven cloth.

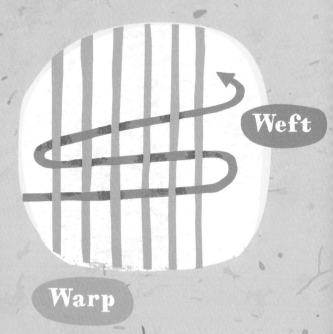

Weft

Warp

Yarn lengths

You will need around 9ft 2in (280cm) of one yarn colour for the warp threads, and several lengths of yarn, each around 20in (50cm), for the weft threads.

You will need

- **Thick cardboard** (around 4 x 6in/10 x 15cm)
- **Pencil**
- **Ruler**
- **Scissors**
- **Yarn** in a few different colours
- **Darning needle** (a blunt needle with a large hole) or you could use a **lolly stick** instead. Wind the yarn around one end of the stick and tape it in place.

1 Use a pencil and ruler to make small marks ½in (1cm) apart along the top and bottom of the cardboard. Snip a small notch at each mark.

2 Now you can attach your warp yarn. Cut a 9ft 2in (280cm) long piece of yarn and slide it through the bottom left notch, leaving an 8in (20cm) long 'tail'. Take the yarn up to the matching slit at the top of the loom, then bring it down the back of the loom to the second slit. Continue winding your yarn all the way around the loom.

3 When you are finished, tie the two ends of the yarn together with a knot at the back of the loom.

4 Now you are ready to start weaving your weft threads. Thread your needle with yarn – around 20in (50cm) is a good length to avoid tangles. Starting at one side of the loom, thread the needle over and under the warp threads. Continue back and forth across the loom to create more rows. After each row, gently push down the yarn using your fingers.

5 When the yarn is nearly run out, finish the row you are on. Then choose a new colour to start the next row. When you finish or start a colour, make sure you leave the ends of the yarn long enough so that you can knot them together later.

6 Keep weaving, changing colour when you like, until your loom is full. Then tie together the pairs of loose ends at the edges of your cloth, using double knots. Snip off the ends.

7 To remove your weaving from the cardboard, cut

through the warp threads at the back of the loom.

8 Finally, tie together all the loose ends at the top and bottom of the cloth, by knotting them in twos. Your weaving is complete!

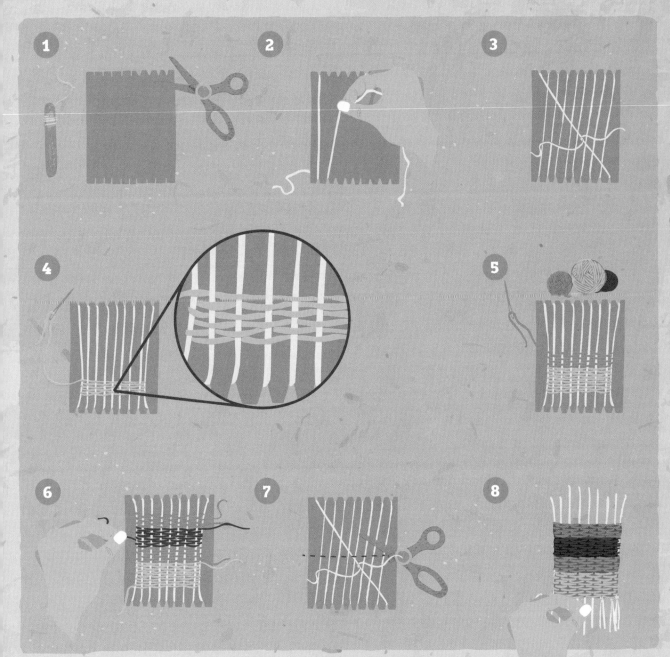

VIKING FASHION

Clothing was a way for people to show off their importance and wealth. Most Vikings wore clothes woven from wool or sometimes flax by the women of the household. The upper classes could afford the luxury of silk, which was imported from Persia and Constantinople.

Looking good

Vikings have a reputation for being scruffy and dirty, but in fact they made an effort to dress well and liked to look good! They dyed their clothes in lots of different colours using plant dyes, and used embroidery, braid and fur trims to decorate them. Both men and women wore jewellery and eye make-up, and styled their hair. Viking men even carried their combs with them on seafaring raids.

Vikings were also pretty clean by the standards of the time. People from other parts of Europe might take a bath just a few times a year, but the Vikings bathed every Saturday on 'laurdag', or 'Washing Day'. The strong homemade soap they used for washing was also used to bleach their hair blond.

Outfit for women

Headscarf

Strap dress, held up by oval brooches (sometimes with beads strung between)

Keys were a status symbol, showing that the woman was in charge of the household.

Comb and case

Underdress, sometimes pleated

Leather shoes

Jewellery

Jewellery was important to the Vikings. They wore arm rings, pendants and brooches made from silver, or from cheaper materials such as bronze or bone. Jewellery was worn for decoration and to show off wealth, but it had a practical purpose too. Brooches were used to fasten clothing, and large pieces of silver jewellery could be cut up into smaller pieces known as 'hack silver' and used as money. Handy!

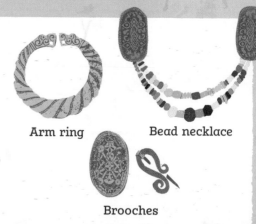

Arm ring

Bead necklace

Brooches

Outfit for men

Cloak fastened with a pin brooch over the shoulder, to keep the sword arm free

[K]yrtill (long [w]ool tunic), [w]orn over an [u]ndertunic

Leather belt, with useful items hung from it (clothes didn't have pockets!)

Trousers were sometimes tight, sometimes baggy.

Some Vikings wore strips of cloth wrapped around the lower part of the leg.

Outfit for a ruler

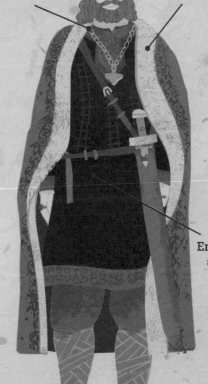

Necklace

Fur cloak

Embroidered silk tunic

Leather shoes

Winter clothing

To keep warm in the chilly Scandinavian winters, Vikings might wear a hood or cap, thick wool socks and cosy mittens made from wool or sheepskin. Animal skins could be treated with beeswax and fish oil to make waterproof clothing that would keep out the rain.

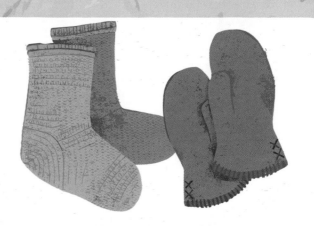

RELIGION AND BELIEFS

Do you believe in magic? The Vikings did! They believed that they shared the world with other beings: powerful gods and goddesses, evil giants, mischievous elves, dwarfs, trolls and other supernatural creatures. Even the natural world was alive, with 'land spirits' dwelling in rocks, air and water.

Many worlds

In Viking mythology, the universe was divided into nine realms or worlds, with a great tree called Yggdrasil at the centre of it. The gods lived in Asgard, which was connected to the human world of Midgard by a rainbow bridge called the Bifrost. Other worlds were home to giants, elves and dwarfs. At the base of Yggdrasil lived the Norns, three women who decided the fate of all creatures. One spun out the thread of each life, another measured its length and the third decided when it should be snapped.

The three Norns

The gods

There were many Viking gods, but some were especially important:

Odin

The most powerful was one-eyed Odin, the god of war, wisdom, magic and poetry. He rode a magical horse with eight legs.

Thor

Thor, the god of thunder, was very strong and not very bright! With the help of his hammer, Mjollnir, he protected Asgard and Midgard.

Odin   Thor

Frey and Freyja

Frey was the god of wealth and good harvests. His sister, Freyja, was the goddess of love and fertility.

Frey   Freyja

Sacrifices and sacred places

The Vikings believed that they needed to keep the gods and other supernatural beings happy. They made offerings of food and drink, and sacrificed animals or sometimes people. In exchange, they hoped for good fortune, such as luck in battle or a successful harvest.

The sacred places where offerings were made were often outdoors, such as in swamps or clearings in the woods. Places where a particular god was honoured were sometimes named after them. In Denmark, for example, the city of Odense (meaning 'Odin's shine') was once a sacred site for Odin.

Days of the week

Some English days of the week are named after Viking gods.

- Tuesday (Tyr's Day). Tyr was the god of war and justice.
- Wednesday (Woden's Day). Woden was another name for Odin.
- Thursday (Thor's Day)
- Friday (Freyja's Day)

From pagan to Christian

Outside of the Viking homelands, some of the most powerful rulers and states in Europe were Christian. As the Vikings raided, settled and traded across Europe, they came into contact with this new religion and gradually began to abandon their old beliefs. By the middle of the 11th century, most Vikings were Christians.

Völva

Sorceresses called Völva carried magic staffs and were believed to have the power to see into the future.

DEATH AND THE AFTERLIFE

The Vikings didn't fear death. For one thing, they thought the time of their death was decided by fate, and so was out of their control. They also believed that a person's life did not end with their last breath, but continued in the afterlife. Bravery in life earned a glorious afterlife!

Lands of the dead

There were several realms in the Viking afterlife. Warriors who died a fearless death in battle might be fortunate enough to end up in Valhalla, Odin's magnificent hall in Asgard. Here, they would spend their days feasting and drinking beer – a warrior's paradise!

Other slain warriors were taken to Fólkvangr, a beautiful meadow that was home to the goddess Freya. Most ordinary Vikings ended up in the underground world of Hel.

Memorial stones

Memorial stones to the dead are found all over the Viking world. Some of these are covered in pictures, and some in runes (the Viking alphabet). One of the best-known memorial stones was raised by King Harald Bluetooth in Jelling in the 10th century, in memory of his parents.

Harald's runestone

Valkyries

Female spirits called Valkyries chose which warriors were worthy of a place in Valhalla and carried them there.

Getting sick

Life was tough in Viking times, and most people only lived until their 40s. Wounds and illnesses that can be easily cured today might well have been fatal back then. The Vikings knew nothing about germs or viruses, and probably blamed illnesses on supernatural beings, such as elves and dwarfs. Illnesses were treated with magic spells and natural plant remedies.

Burials

Funerals were important rituals. Vikings believed they allowed the dead person to move on to the afterlife. People were buried in lots of different ways. Some Vikings were cremated, while others were buried in coffins, underground chambers, wagons or boats. Some were even buried sitting upright in chairs. Graves were placed close to settlements, and often marked by mounds of earth or stones.

The dead were often surrounded by possessions to take with them into the afterlife: weapons, shields, tools, cooking utensils and jewellery.

Ships were valuable and took a long time to build. The more important the person, the bigger the ship they might be buried in.

Some burial ships were set on fire, while others were covered with a mound of earth.

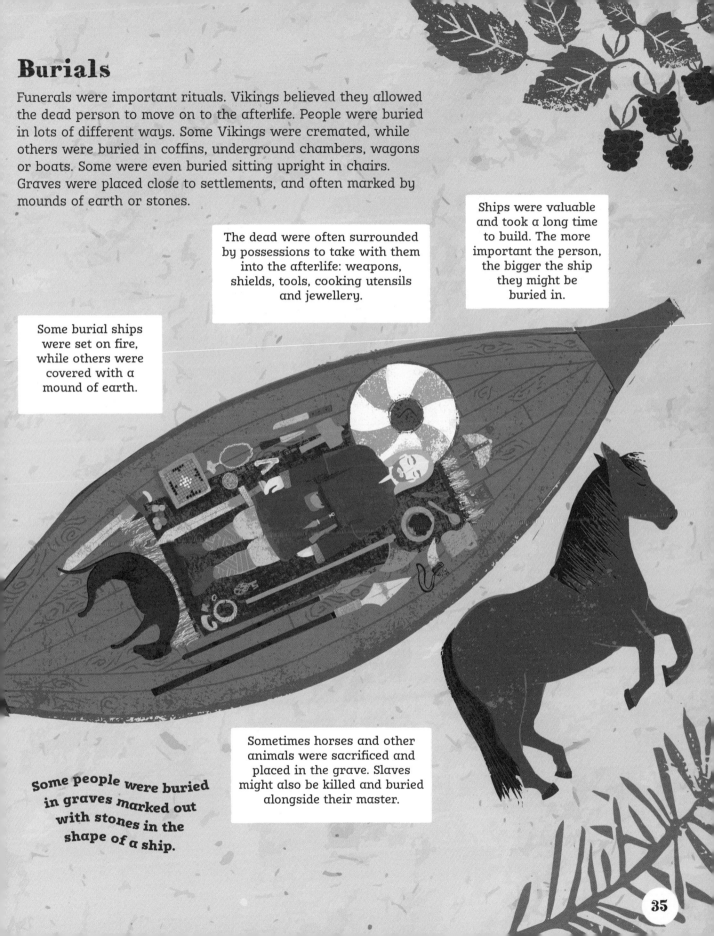

Sometimes horses and other animals were sacrificed and placed in the grave. Slaves might also be killed and buried alongside their master.

Some people were buried in graves marked out with stones in the shape of a ship.

MAKE A THOR'S HAMMER PENDANT

Some Vikings wore amulets (lucky charms) around their necks to ward off illness or bad luck. Amulets shaped like Thor's hammer were especially popular. Who wouldn't want the mighty thunder god on their side? Try making your own Thor's hammer pendant, just like a Viking!

You will need

- **air-dry clay** (small piece about the size of a coin)
- **pencil**
- **blunt knife** or toothpick, for mark-making
- **gold acrylic paint**
- **paintbrush**
- **yarn** in 3 different colours, each around 3ft (1m) long
- **sticky tape**

1 Roll the clay into a ball, then squash it flat.

2 Use your fingers to squeeze the sides of the clay inwards, to make a rough cross shape. When done, squash the clay flat again.

3 Keep shaping the pendant to give it a V-shaped bottom and a taller 'neck'. When you are happy with the shape, use a pencil to make a hole in the neck of the pendant. Make sure the pencil fits all the way through.

4 Draw a simple design on your pendant, using the point of the pencil and a blunt knife or toothpick. You could make dots, lines or swirls. Leave the clay to dry.

5 Once dry, paint the pendant using gold acrylic paint. Leave to dry.

6 To make the cord for your necklace, take the three

lengths of yarn and knot them together at one end. Tape them to a surface using sticky tape, and separate the strands so they are not overlapping.

7 Now plait the yarn. To start, bring the left strand over the central strand so that it is in the centre....

... and then bring the right strand across the new central stand so that it is in the centre.

8 Repeat this pattern, bringing first one and then the other outside strand to the centre. Once you have used up all the yarn, tie the ends together in a knot.

9 Thread your pendant onto the cord and tie the two ends of the cord together. Your pendant is ready to wear – may the might of Thor be with you!

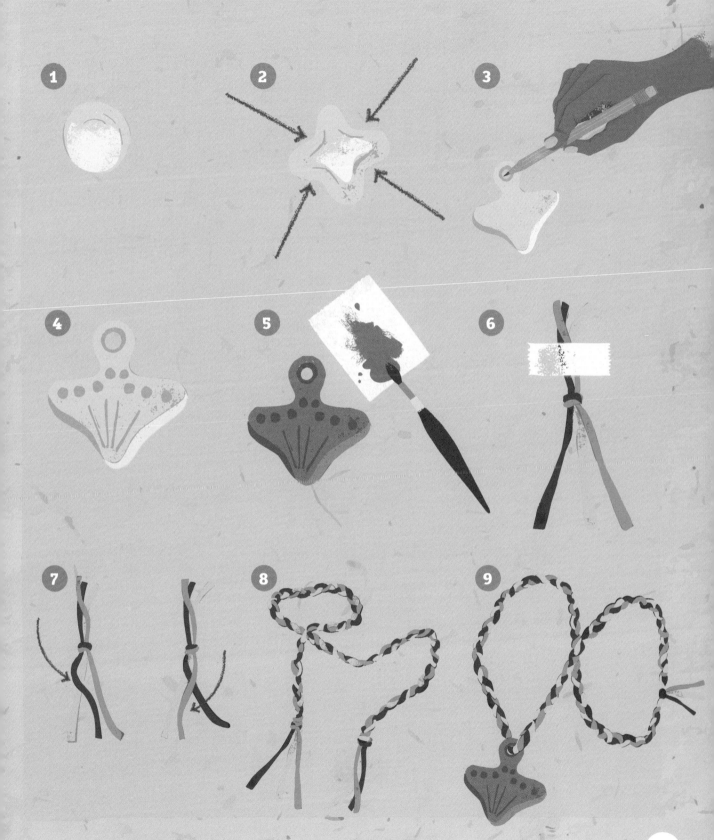

A VIKING BURIAL

Today is an important day. Grim Redbeard has died and everyone in our village has gathered to send him on his way to the next life. Grim became ill with a fever not long after harvest time. His family tried to save him – my friend Inga says they sacrificed six chickens and a goat. But Grim just got sicker and sicker. My mother says it must have been his time to die. I heard my father say he was unlucky not to fall in battle. Grim was a great warrior and my father always hoped he and his friend would one day feast together in the golden hall at Valhalla.

Our village's burial place is not far from my home, just beyond the barley field. My aunt's grave is here, marked by a single standing stone. Grim's resting place will be far grander though. This winter, the men of the village will gather huge stones to form the shape of a mighty ship that will carry him to the afterlife!

Today though, Grim is laid out on a blanket on top of a huge pyre of wood. He looks magnificent. Grim's wife and daughters have been working for days, from sunrise to nightfall, to sew him a fine new tunic and a cloak trimmed with fur. His head rests on his shield and his hands are folded around his trusty axe. At his feet I can see the knife that he once used to carve me a little wooden horse. Beside it is his comb, some dice, spoons, dishes and cooking pans – Grim loved his food! I watch as his eldest son, Bjorn, carefully places a drinking horn at his father's side. Now Grim will be able to drink as much beer as he likes with his friends in the afterlife.

People begin to play flutes and lyres, and lift their voices in song as loud as thunder. Beer and wooden bowls piled high with roasted meat are passed around. The whole village has been cooking for days to prepare a feast worthy of the great Grim. My father and the other men lift their drinking horns to their lips again and again, until they are swaying. When the sun dips down behind the hill, a bleating goat is led up to the pyre, ready to be sacrificed and laid beside Grim.

The light is beginning to fade now. It's time to light the torches. Our faces flicker in the glowing torchlight as we gather around the pyre, chanting softly. Bjorn approaches first and thrusts his flaming torch into the pyre. One by one, we all do the same. The wood crackles as it begins to catch and the dancing flames spread. Farewell Grim Redbeard! May the smoke and fire carry you safely to your glorious next life in the world of the dead.

MAKE A RUNE NAME SIGN

Runes are the letters that the Vikings used to write down their language, Old Norse. They were not written on paper, but were carved onto stone, wood and bone. Have a go at carving runes yourself, and make a name sign for your room.

You will need

- **air-dry clay** 3½oz (100g)
- **rolling pin**
- **blunt knife**
- **blunt pencil**
- **acrylic paints**
- **paintbrush**
- **length of string** 12in (30cm)

1 Roll out the clay to a thickness of around ³⁄₁₆in (0.5cm). Use a blunt knife to trim the edges into a rough rectangle with curved corners.

2 Use a pencil to carve a simple design around the border, leaving the central area blank. Make two holes at the top of the sign by pushing the pencil all the way through the clay.

3 In the centre of the sign, carve the runes that make up your name (on the page opposite). If any of the letters in your name doesn't have a matching rune, just use the letter or combination of letters with the closest sound – for example, for D use T, for E use I, for G use K, for O use U, and for X use K and S. Leave the clay to dry (this will take several days).

4 Paint your sign and leave it to dry.

5 Thread string through the holes. Your name sign is ready to hang!

Runes were made up of straight lines, which made them easier to carve.

Writing with runes

The Vikings did not write down very much. Their stories, histories and laws were passed on by word-of-mouth instead, from one generation to the next. When they did write things down, it was often for practical purposes, such as labelling belongings or writing business letters. Runes were also carved onto objects to give them 'magical' powers, such as protection from illness, and were used to record the achievements of the dead on memorial stones (see page 34).

This comb case was found in England. The runes on it say 'Thorfast made a good comb'.

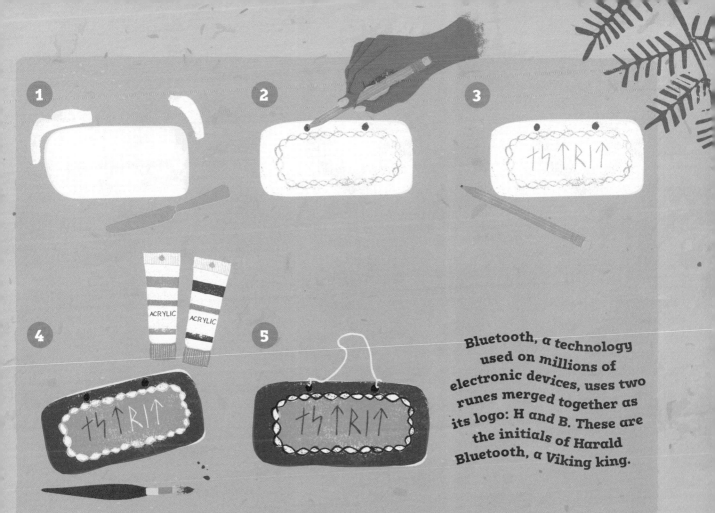

Bluetooth, a technology used on millions of electronic devices, uses two runes merged together as its logo: H and B. These are the initials of Harald Bluetooth, a Viking king.

The Futhark alphabet

The rune alphabet is called 'futhark,' after the first six letters in it: f, u, l, th (a single letter), a, r, and k. Different versions of the futhark alphabet were used in different times and in different regions. The futhark used during most of the Viking Age had 16 letters.

Runes weren't just letters. Each rune also had a special meaning too; for example, ᚠ meant 'wealth' and ᛚ meant 'sea'.

FUN AND GAMES

Viking life wasn't all fighting and farming – people had time for fun, too. They played board games and ball games, competed against each other in sporting contests, and enjoyed feasts, where they drank, sang and listened to stories of Viking heroes.

Board games

Just like us, Vikings liked to play board games. Archaeologists have found beautifully carved wooden game boards and delicate gaming pieces made from glass, antler and other materials. Hnefatafl was a strategy game a bit like chess. No one knows the exact rules, but the overall aim was for one side to attack and capture the other side's king.

Telling stories

The Vikings loved listening to stories and poems about brave Viking heroes, gods and goddesses, great battles and perilous sea voyages. These stories, called sagas, were told from memory and passed on from one generation to the next. After the Viking Age had ended, writers heard the stories and wrote them down, which is how we know about them today. How well do you think they remembered the stories they wrote down?

Chieftains and kings had their own poets, called skalds, whose job it was to make up poems praising their master's strength and bravery.

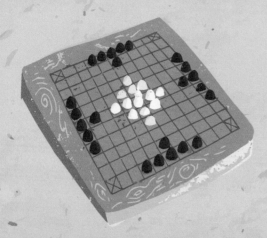

Kennings

Many Norse poems used 'kennings' – two-word phrases that describe people, places or things in an unusual way, without actually naming them. For example, one poem describes the sea as a 'sail-road' and a throne as a 'treasure-seat'.

Outdoor sports

Playing outdoor games helped men stay fit and strong. Men showed off their strength in wrestling matches, stone-lifting contests and ball games like knattleikr, a rough contact game that involved teams throwing and chasing a ball. They also practiced important skills like archery, spear throwing and sword-fighting.

As well as wrestling and fighting each other, Vikings liked to set up fights between stallions (male horses). These violent events attracted spectators from far and wide.

Party time

Feasts were held to celebrate weddings, victories in battle, and other special occasions. They were a way for a chieftain to reward his men and make sure they stayed loyal to him. Feasts could last for days. Women played an important role preparing and serving the food. People sang and danced, played board and dice games, listened to stories and drank a lot of ale and mead!

FOOD AND DRINK

Viking families spent a lot of their time making sure they had enough to eat. Some food could be bought from markets or bartered (swapped) with others, but most of it had to be reared, caught or grown by themselves. How exhausting!

What Vikings ate

Most people ate a simple diet of bread, porridge, eggs, fish, cheese, fruit and vegetables, with a little bit of meat from time to time. Food was washed down with water, milk, beer or mead.

Cooking and eating

In a Viking home, there would generally be a big pot of something bubbling away on the hearth. Stews were cooked in a cauldron, a big pot made of iron or soapstone, which was hung on a chain from the ceiling or from a tripod.

People generally ate two meals a day: a 'day-meal' (dagmal) when they woke up, and a 'night-meal' (nattmal) in the early evening. They used wooden bowls and plates, and ate with their hands and a sharp knife.

The Vikings didn't have potatoes, tomatoes or corn. All of these foods arrived in Europe much later.

Preserve food, like a Viking!

To make sure they had enough to eat in the winter, the Vikings preserved some foods by smoking, salting or pickling them or hanging them in the open air to dry. You can have a go at drying apples. You'll need a few days of hot, sunny weather. With an adult's help, wash, core and thinly slice your apples, and squeeze over some lemon juice to stop them from browning. Place them on a baking rack and cover with a tea towel. Leave them outside in the sun for 2–3 days, turning them occasionally and bringing them in at night.

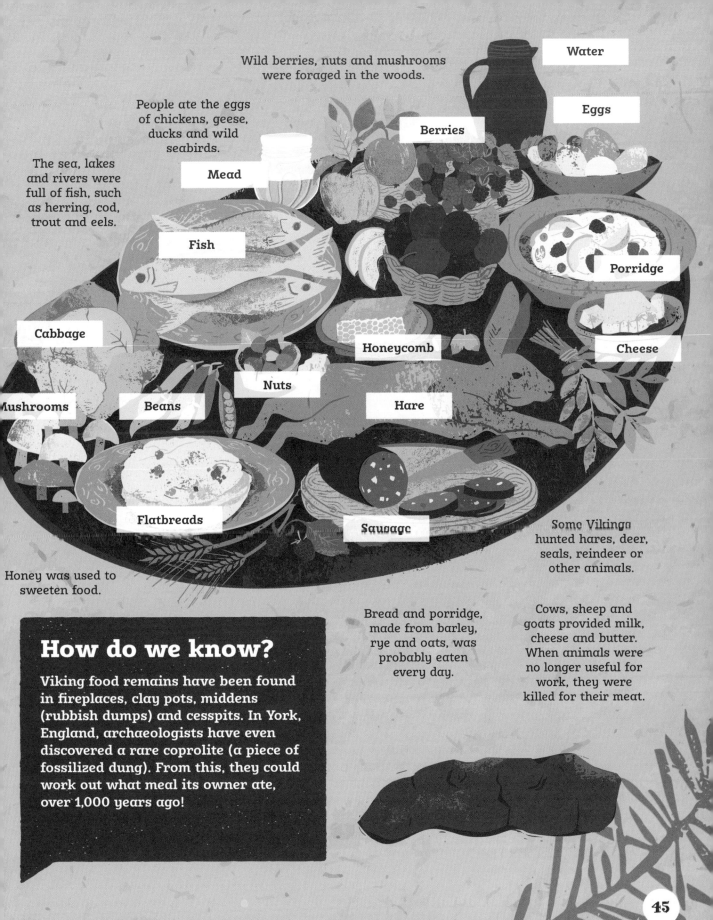

Wild berries, nuts and mushrooms were foraged in the woods.

Water

People ate the eggs of chickens, geese, ducks and wild seabirds.

Eggs

Berries

Mead

The sea, lakes and rivers were full of fish, such as herring, cod, trout and eels.

Fish

Porridge

Cabbage

Cheese

Honeycomb

Nuts

Mushrooms

Beans

Hare

Flatbreads

Sausage

Some Vikings hunted hares, deer, seals, reindeer or other animals.

Honey was used to sweeten food.

Bread and porridge, made from barley, rye and oats, was probably eaten every day.

Cows, sheep and goats provided milk, cheese and butter. When animals were no longer useful for work, they were killed for their meat.

How do we know?

Viking food remains have been found in fireplaces, clay pots, middens (rubbish dumps) and cesspits. In York, England, archaeologists have even discovered a rare coprolite (a piece of fossilized dung). From this, they could work out what meal its owner ate, over 1,000 years ago!

MAKE A VIKING DRINKING HORN

Most of the time, Vikings drank from cups made of wood or pottery but special occasions might call for something grander: a drinking horn! These were made from hollowed-out cattle horns, and sometimes beautifully decorated. Why not make some mead (see page 51), and drink it from your home-made drinking horn?

You will need

- **paper cup**
- **sheets of card** 2–3 A4 (letter-size)
- **Stapler**
- **Sticky tape**
- **PVA glue**
- **Old newspaper**
- **White and brown paint**
- **Paintbrush**
- **1 sheet gold card**
- **length of string** (optional) 50in (120cm)

You can use your drinking horn again and again. Just try not to get the outside wet when you wash it up afterwards.

1 Cut a wide strip of card and wrap it around the bottom of the cup to form a cylinder. Use sticky tape to attach it to the cup.

2 Turn the cup over, so that the cylinder is at the top. Roll up another strip of card and staple the ends together to make a cylinder that is just small enough to fit inside the cylinder on the cup. Slot it in, at a slight angle, and secure with staples or sticky tape.

3 Continue making cylinders, each one smaller than the one before. As you attach each one, try to create a curved shape by angling the cylinders over to one side. Don't worry about any small gaps – you will be covering these up in the next step. You will probably need at least 12 cylinders in total.

4 Once your horn is finished, you can cover it in papier mâché. Be prepared to get messy! Cover your work area in newspaper, and tear some more newspaper into long strips. In a container, mix together two parts PVA glue with one part water to make a runny glue. Dip a strip of newspaper into the glue mixture, then remove any excess glue by running your fingers down the strip. Wrap the strip around the horn, using your fingers to smooth any bumps.

5 Continue applying strips of newspaper until all of the horn is covered. Leave it to dry (this will take around a day).

6 Once the horn is completely dry, it's ready for painting. Mix a little bit of brown paint into white paint to make an off-white colour, then paint the outside of the horn.

7 Once the horn is dry, cut a strip of gold card and glue it around the rim. Add another gold band near the bottom of the horn. If you like, tie a piece of string onto the horn so that you can wear it round your neck. Your drinking horn is ready to use!

THE TALE OF THOR'S STOLEN HAMMER

The sun has dipped below the hills and the sky is growing dark. I snuggle down under my furs, warm and drowsy. Father has promised to tell us a story, and soon his deep, rumbling voice fills the room...

"One morning, as the bright sun-candle rose in the sky, Thor awoke, to find all was not well. Mjölnir, his mighty hammer, was missing from his side. Though he searched through all of Asgard, Mjölnir was nowhere to be found. Greatly upset, he sought the help of Loki, who said he thought he knew where the hammer might be found.

Together they went to Freyja, the most beautiful goddess in Asgard, and asked to borrow her magical cloak of feathers. Loki slipped it on, and with the whistling wings of a bird he rose and flew though the skies to Jotunheim, the land of the giants. Here, he found Thyrm, the king of the Frost-Giants, who confessed he had stolen Mjölnir. He would only return it, he said, if Freyja agreed to be his bride.

When Loki returned to Asgard and delivered Thyrm's message, Thor insisted that Freyja do as Thyrm commanded. But Freyja refused and flew into such a towering rage that the halls of Asgard trembled! The gods and goddesses held a council to make a plan. Heimdal, the wise watchman god, had an idea. Why didn't Thor dress up as Freyja and return to Jotunheim in disguise? Thor was indignant. The mighty Thor dress as a woman? It was unmanly!"

At this point in the story, my younger brother starts giggling. This story is his favourite.

"Finally," my father continues once the giggles have died down, "Thor agreed. Wearing a long wedding gown and a veil over his face, he returned to Jotunheim, with Loki disguised as his maid. That evening, a great wedding feast was held. As was his custom, Thor ate heartily, devouring an entire ox and three whole barrels of mead. Thyrm was startled by his lovely bride's enormous appetite, but clever Loki knew just what to say. 'Your bride is so excited to be married', he said, 'she had not eaten for eight days'.

Eager to kiss his bride, Thyrm lifted Thor's veil, only to spring back in horror at the sight of two terrifying red eyes, burning with fire! Again, Loki's quick tongue came to the rescue. 'Your bride is so impatient to be married', he said, 'she has not slept for eight nights'.

Finally, Thrym commanded that Mjölnir be brought forth and placed in his bride's lap to bless the marriage. As soon as Thor set eyes on Mjölnir, his heart laughed within him. Seizing it, he swung it around his head and knocked Thrym to the ground, splitting his skull in two. Soon, all the giants in the hall lay dead beside their king. Thor, slayer of giants, had avenged the theft of his hammer."

VIKING RECIPES

The Viking diet was pretty healthy, with lots of vegetables and berries, grains and fish. Do you think you would have enjoyed eating and drinking like a Viking? Try out these recipes and see.

Flatbread

Flatbreads were grilled on a hot stone or baked in a pan over the fire. Sometimes they were sweetened with honey. Bread was often made with barley flour but this recipe uses wheat flour, which is easier to get hold of.

Makes 4 flatbreads

You will need

- 3½oz (100g) bread flour
- 3½oz (100g) wholemeal flour
- 2 tbsp butter or yoghurt
- 3½fl oz (100ml) lukewarm water
- ¼ tsp salt

1 In a bowl, mix all the ingredients together to form a dough, then knead for 2–3 minutes. If the dough is too dry, add more water. If it's too wet, add more flour.

2 Leave the dough to rest in the bowl covered by a tea towel for 1 hour.

3 Divide the dough into four. Use a rolling pin to roll each piece into a disc around ³⁄₁₆in (0.5cm) thick.

4 Heat up a heavy frying pan (you don't need any oil). Cook the flatbreads for around 4 minutes on each side until they are golden brown.

Pea and spring onion soup

The Vikings cooked a lot of their food by boiling it in a big pot on the hearth. This soup is made using some of the vegetables the Vikings would have eaten.

Serves 4 | **Adult help required** |

You will need

- 3½oz (100g) spring onions, roughly chopped
- 10½oz (300g) frozen peas
- 1 clove garlic, crushed
- 1 tbsp butter
- 23½fl oz (700ml) hot vegetable stock

1 Melt the butter in a saucepan, then gently fry the spring onion and garlic for 3–4 minutes. Add the peas and cook for another 2 minutes.

2 Add the hot vegetable stock, bring to the boil and simmer for 10 minutes. Season with salt and pepper and leave to cool slightly.

3 Blend the soup until it is smooth, then serve.

Mead

Mead, an alcoholic drink made from water and fermented honey, was much loved by the Vikings. Herbs, fruits, or spices were added for extra flavour. The recipe here is a non-alcoholic version.

Serves 4 | **Adult help required**

You will need

- 17fl oz (500ml) water
- 6½fl oz (200ml) honey
- 3½fl oz (100ml) apple juice
- ¼ tsp each of cinnamon, cloves, nutmeg and ginger (optional)

1 Add all the ingredients to a saucepan, bring to the boil and simmer gently for 5 minutes. Leave to cool slightly before drinking.

Porridge with berries

Vikings probably ate a lot of porridge. It was made from barley, oats or other grains, and had berries or apples mixed in to add sweetness.

Serves 4 | **Adult help required**

You will need

- 3½oz (100g) pearl barley
- 2oz (50g) rolled oats
- 13½–20fl oz (400–600ml) water
- 3½fl oz (100ml) milk
- ¼ tsp salt
- Honey
- Hazelnuts, roasted and chopped
- Fruit, such as chopped apples, berries, or dried cranberries

1 Add the pearl barley, oats, water and salt to a saucepan and bring the boil. Simmer on a low heat for around 45 minutes, adding extra water if the porridge becomes too thick.

2 Once the pearl barley is cooked (it should be tender but still chewy), add the milk.

3 Serve the porridge topped with honey, hazelnuts and fruit.

COULD YOU LIVE LIKE A VIKING?

The Viking way of life was very different to ours. Most people lived in tiny communities, and day-to-day life was pretty tough. Do you think you would like to live like a Viking? Think about the questions here and talk about your answers with a friend, parent, carer or teacher.

1 Instead of going to school, Viking children helped out at home, learning skills they would need as adults, like farming, foraging, fighting, cooking, woodwork and making clothes. Do you think you would enjoy a childhood like this? Which Viking skill would you most like to learn? What would you miss most about school?

2 The Vikings were great explorers. How do you think you would feel setting sail into uncharted oceans, with no idea if you would find land or not? Imagine discovering an uninhabited island and setting up the very first settlement there. How would you build a shelter? What would you eat and drink? Where would you choose to build your farm?

3 Law-breakers in the Viking Age were punished in different ways. They might have to pay a fine, become a slave and work for their victim, or be outlawed from the community to live (and probably die) in the wilderness. If you were part of a Viking community judging the crimes below, what punishment might you give each one?

- Stealing a neighbour's cow
- Burning down a neighbour's house
- Injuring a person in a fight

4 Viking children had very few toys, so had to make their own entertainment. Can you use your imagination to think up a game that you could play using some or all of these items: pebbles, a wooden bowl, some sticks?

5 Not all Vikings lives were the same. Which of the following would you rather be?

- A Viking chieftain – you live for glory and don't fear danger.
- A trader sailing to Constantinople, the greatest city in Europe.
- A woman in a small farming settlement – you spend your time cooking, making clothes and looking after your family.
- A blacksmith – you're well-respected, but it's hot, hard work.
- A skald (storyteller) – you'll need to have a good memory, and be able to think on your feet.
- A settler setting sail with your husband to new lands across the ocean – who knows what lies ahead?

6 In the Viking Age, everything had to be made by hand, and it all took time. Think of a simple slice of bread with butter. To make this, a Viking would need to grow some wheat, harvest it, mill it into flour, make bread dough, cook it over a fire (burning wood they had chopped themselves), milk a cow and churn the cream to make butter. Phew – that's a lot of work! Think about your favourite meal. Can you think of all the different jobs a Viking might need to do to make it?

7 If you time-travelled back to Viking times, what three things do you think you would miss the most from your modern-day life? It might be certain gadgets, toys or foods, things you like to do, or comforts like a comfy bed! Is there anything you'd like to take from the time of the Vikings and bring back to the modern world?

GLOSSARY

afterlife
A place where some people believe you go after death.

archaeologist
A person who studies how humans lived in the past by looking at the things they left behind, such as pottery, tools and buildings.

Asgard
The mythical home of the Norse gods.

burial mound
A hill of earth and stones built over a grave.

cesspit
Hole in the ground used for human waste.

chainmail
Armour made from small metal rings linked together to form a mesh.

chieftain
The wealthy and powerful leader of a local area, also known as a 'jarl'. They commanded the loyalty of the men in their community.

cremate
To burn a dead person's body.

figurehead
A carved figure or symbol decorating the bow (front) of a ship.

fjord
A long, narrow inlet of the sea surrounded by steep cliffs. Fjords are created by glaciers.

forage
To wander and search for wild things to eat (such as berries or mushrooms) or use.

futhark
The Viking alphabet. The 'Elder Futhark' alphabet was used up until around the 8th century and had 24 runes. It was replaced by the 'Younger Futhark', which had 16 runes. The Younger Futhark came in

different versions: 'long branch' runes were used in Denmark, while 'short twig' runes were used in Sweden and Norway.

hoard
A collection of treasure buried for safe-keeping.

homestead
A farmhouse and the surrounding land and other buildings.

longhouse
A long, narrow, single-room building where many people all live and sleep together.

longship
A long, narrow ship powered by a large square sail and many oars.

loot
To steal money or treasure. The word is also used to describe the goods that are stolen.

memorial stone
A stone carved with writing and pictures, which was raised in memory of the dead. Memorial stones are also known as 'rune stones'.

merchant
A person who travels from place to place, buying and selling goods.

migrate
To move permanently from one place to another. Some Vikings migrated to new lands, looking for better farmland and an easier life.

monastery
A place where a religious community of people such as monks or nuns live and work. The Vikings raided many monasteries because they were wealthy and often undefended.

navigate
To find a way across water or land.

pagan
A person who belongs to a religion that is not one of the main world religions. Pagans believe in many gods.

plough
A large tool used by farmers to loosen and turn over the soil before seeds are planted.

quern-stone
A round stone used for milling (grinding) grain into flour. They were used in pairs: the upper stone was moved around to grind against the lower stone.

ritual
A ceremony made up of a sequence of actions or words performed in a certain way.

runes
The letters used to write the Old Norse language. They could be written left to right, or right to left. See also 'futhark'.

sagas
Stories about Viking people, gods and events that are spoken aloud and handed down by word-of-mouth for centuries. They were written down long after the Viking Age had ended, mainly in Iceland in the 12th and 13th centuries. The sagas help to give us an idea of what Viking life might have been like, but we can't believe everything that is written in them.

scabbard
A holder for a sword or knife.

settler
A person who moves to a new land to live.

sickle
A tool with a short handle and a long, curved blade used for cutting grass, corn and other crops.

skald
A poet who composed, memorized and performed epic poems about kings and heroes. Skalds were important, honoured people in Viking society.

slave
A woman, man or child who is owned as property by someone else, and made to work.

smithy
A place where a blacksmith works.

spindle
A tool used to twist wool and turn it into thread.

textile
Woven or knitted cloth.

turf
The upper layer of grass and soil, held together by roots.

Thing
Local assembly where free men regularly gathered to make decisions and solve disputes.

ABOUT THE AUTHOR

Claire Saunders has been writing and editing books for more than 20 years. Specialising in children's non-fiction, she has authored or co-authored many titles including *Live Like a Roman* (for Button Books), *The Power Book*, *The Birthday Almanac*, *A World of Gratitude* and various activity books, including *The Great British Staycation Activity Book*, the *Football Fantastic Activity Book* and the *Only in America Activity Book*. A graduate of Cambridge University, she has previously worked for Ivy Press and Rough Guides and still loves travelling the world, learning about the history of other cultures. She lives with her family in Lewes, southern England.

Acknowledgements

Thanks to Dr Steve Ashby for his expert knowledge and help.

First published 2024 by Button Books, an imprint of Guild of Master Craftsman Publications Ltd, Castle Place, 166 High Street, Lewes, East Sussex, BN7 1XU, UK. Text © Claire Saunders, 2024. Copyright in the Work © GMC Publications Ltd, 2024. ISBN 978 1 78708 137 6. Distributed by Publishers Group West in the United States. All rights reserved. The right of Claire Saunders to be identified as the author of this work has been asserted in accordance with the Copyright, Designs and Patents Act 1988, sections 77 and 78. No part of this publication may be reproduced, stored in a retrieval system, or transmitted in any form or by any means without the prior permission of the publisher and copyright owner. The publishers and author can accept no legal responsibility for any consequences arising from the application of information, advice, or instructions given in this publication. A catalogue record for this book is available from the British Library. Publisher: Jonathan Bailey, Production: Jim Bulley, Senior Project Editor: Susie Behar, Designer: Robin Shields, Illustrator: Ruth Hickson. Colour origination by GMC Reprographics. Printed and bound in China.

FSC
www.fsc.org
MIX
Paper | Supporting responsible forestry
FSC® C020056

Button Books

For more on Button Books, contact:
GMC Publications Ltd, Castle Place,
166 High Street, Lewes, East Sussex,
BN7 1XU, United Kingdom
Tel: +44 (0)1273 488005
buttonbooks.co.uk/buttonbooks.us